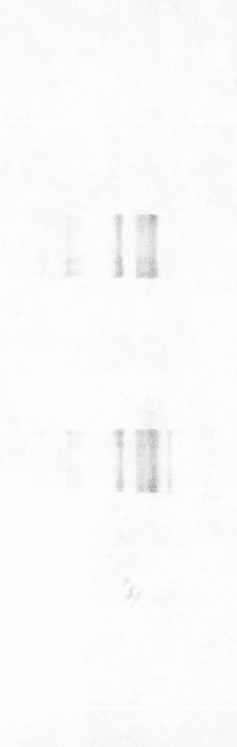

Baseball

SUPERSTARS

by Mike Herbert

CHILDRENS PRESS®

CHICAGO

To the Reader

Included in this book are facts about twenty-five baseball superstars. They are presented in alphabetical order. You may not agree with our choices. You may have a favorite who is not included. However, we still hope you will enjoy reading about these stars and the major league baseball teams of the National and American Leagues.

Photo Credits

Sissac—4, 30; Minnesota Twins—6; Peter Travers—8, 10, 38; Ira Golden—12, 16, 22, 28, 32, 52; G. Robarge—14, 18, 44, 46, 50; Nancy Hogue—20; Vic Milton—24; George Gojkovich—26, 40; Dave Kingdon—Cover, 34, 48; Ray DeAragon—36; Kansas City Royals—42; © Major League Baseball Promotion Corporation—58, 59, 60, 61, 62, 63, 64

Cover and interior design by Karen A. Yops

Library of Congress Cataloging in Publication Data

Herbert, Mike.
  Baseball superstars.

  Summary: Presents brief profiles of twenty-five major league baseball stars and includes a history of the world series and the National and American Leagues.
  1. Baseball players—United States—Biography—Juvenile literature. [1. baseball players.] I. Title.
GV865.A1H47 1986   796.357′092′2 [B] [920] 85-29991
ISBN 0-516-04434-6

1 2 3 4 5 6 7 8 9 10 R 95 94 93 92 91 90 89 88 87 86

CONTENTS

HAROLD BAINES
outfielder
Chicago White Sox

Born March 15, 1959 in Easton, Maryland
Attended St. Michael's High School.

Harold Baines is a very quiet, soft-spoken man. If he weren't a major league baseball player, very few people would notice him.

Bill Veeck was a baseball team owner. He once owned the Chicago White Sox.

Both Baines and Veeck lived on Maryland's Eastern Shore. When Harold was only 12 years old he was "discovered" by Bill Veeck. The owner said the boy could play someday in the major leagues. Later, after Harold had been a spectacular high school baseball and basketball player, the Chicago White Sox followed Veeck's advice and picked Harold as the No. 1 player in the 1977 draft.

Three years later, Harold arrived in Chicago. He proved Bill Veeck right. He became the White Sox' best left-handed home run hitter.

A .300 HITTER—Harold has hit more than .300 for the past two years—the only White Sox regular player to do so. He is still soft-spoken, but everyone knows who Harold Baines is now.

BERT BLYLEVEN
pitcher
Minnesota Twins

Born April 6, 1951 in Zeist, Holland

Major league baseball pitchers throw lots of different pitches to try to fool batters. The most popular pitch is the fastball. Some pitchers can throw a fastball almost 100 miles per hour.

By flipping his wrist and fingers as he throws the ball, the pitcher puts spin on the ball and makes the ball go right over the plate, then curve just as the batter tries to hit it.

Bert Blyleven has learned to throw a curve better than almost anyone. Using that pitch more than any other, he has won many, many games. He has a very low earned run average (about 3.00), and more than 2,800 strikeouts.

In 1977, against the California Angels, he pitched a no-hitter! And many times, more than a dozen, he has pitched complete game shutouts.

BORN IN HOLLAND—Bert Blyleven was born in Holland and moved to the United States when he was about six years old. He grew up in Southern California and after just 21 minor league games he joined the major leagues. His full name is Rik Aalbert Blyleven.

WADE BOGGS
third baseman
Boston Red Sox

Born June 15, 1958 in Omaha, Nebraska
Attended H.B. Plant High School in Tampa,
Florida.

Nickname: Bogus

Wade Boggs always worked hard to be a good
baseball player. He learned from his father, from
his friends, from Little League and Legion baseball
coaches, and he played six years in the minors
before he came to the Boston Red Sox in 1982.

Wade learned well. Today he is considered one
of the smartest hitters in baseball. He knows what
it takes to hit a baseball. Now he is a great hitter.
In 1983 he hit .361; in 1984, .325; in 1985, .368—
the best in all major league baseball!

Boggs' best friend in baseball is also a great-
hitting third baseman: George Brett of the Kansas
City Royals. The two players like each other very
much. They try to beat each other and do better
than each other all the time.

THE PERFECT HITTER—Boggs is a perfect
hitter. He has a balanced stance, ready to hit any
pitch. He has a disciplined strike zone, he doesn't
swing at bad pitches. And, he keeps his head low
so he can see the pitches.

GEORGE BRETT
third baseman
Kansas City Royals

Born May 15, 1953 in Glendale, West Virginia
Attended El Segundo (California) High School.

George Brett grew up in a family that loved baseball. His father pushed him into being a player. He also pushed George's brother, Ken. Both Ken and George made the major leagues.

But George was the better player, and he has become one of the greatest players in baseball history. For the last 10 years he has dominated the game—setting records and proving himself to be a star. He is a fine fielder, but he is a better hitter. He hits home runs, and he also hits for a high average. Since he became the Royals third baseman in 1974, for the year he has hit .282, .308, .333, .312, .294, .329, .390, .314, .301, .310, .284, and .335. In 1976 and 1980 his average led the league. And when his team has played in the World Series, he has hit even better.

A CLUTCH PERFORMER—George comes through in the clutch. He is the player all his teammates look to for inspiration. When George hits, his team wins. In the 1985 World Series, he almost single-handedly led the Royals to victory, hitting home runs and key hits when the team needed him. George Brett is a winner.

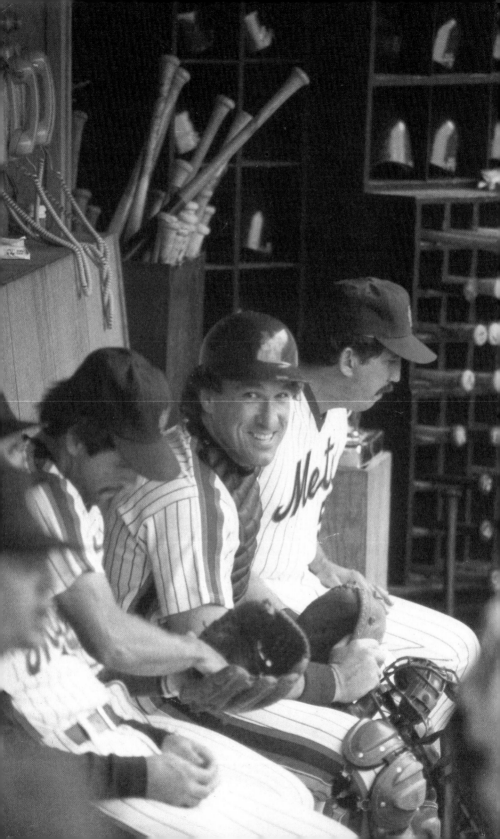

GARY CARTER
catcher
New York Mets

Born April 8, 1954 in Culver City, California
Attended Sunnyhills High School in Fullerton,
California.

Nickname: The Kid

Gary Carter was always a great athlete. In high
school he was the captain of his baseball, football,
and basketball teams as a junior and as a senior.
He was also a great student. He was a member of
the National Honor Society, near the top of his
class. And UCLA wanted him to go to school there
and play quarterback on their football team.

But Gary decided to play baseball instead.

In 1975, after three years in the minors, he
came to the Montreal Expos and soon became the
starting catcher. That year he was the Expos Player
of the Year and the league's Rookie of the Year.

TRADED—After 10 years in Montreal, Carter
was traded to the New York Mets in 1985. How
did he do? He led the team in home runs with 32
and runs-batted-in with 100. Carter was still a
star, even though he had had a knee operation the
year before. "It's the same knee I injured playing
high school football," he said. "The way I feel now,
I could catch 10 more years."

CARLTON FISK
catcher
Chicago White Sox

Born December 26, 1947 in Bellow Falls,
Vermont
  Attended Charlestown (New Hampshire) High
School and the University of New Hampshire.

Nickname: Pudge

The hardest-working player on a baseball team
is the catcher. Pitchers work hard when they pitch,
but they don't play every day. Catchers have to do
it every day.

Carlton first played with the Boston Red Sox.
He was the American League Rookie of the Year in
1973, batting .293 with 22 home runs, and he won
a Gold Glove fielding award. In 1981 Fisk moved to
the Chicago White Sox and in two years he had
helped make the team division champions.

With 257 home runs, Fisk is the third-best
home run hitting catcher in baseball history,
behind Yogi Berra and No. 1 Johnny Bench.

A CLUTCH HITTER—Carlton Fisk's greatest
hit was a home run in the 12th inning to win the
sixth game of the 1975 World Series against the
Cincinnati Reds in Boston's Fenway Park.

DWIGHT GOODEN
pitcher
New York Mets

Born November 16, 1964 in Tampa, Florida
Attended Hillsborough (Tampa) High School.

Nickname: Doc or Doctor K

Dwight Gooden's father, Dan, always loved
baseball. He always went to baseball games—
especially during spring training in Florida.

When Dwight was only four years old, Dan
started taking him to games, too. Dwight learned
to love baseball.

Dwight was always good, but never the best.
There was always another pitcher better. Until
1984, however. That's when Dwight, only 19 years
old, became a New York Met. Then he proved he
was the best. He struck out 276 batters! He won
17 games. Everyone was talking about the great
young star, the youngest National League Rookie
of the Year ever. He set or tied 15 records!

NO SOPHOMORE JINX—Sometimes players
are great their first year, then they don't do as
well. Dwight Gooden was better his second year,
1985, than his first. He won 24 games! He allowed
the least runs of any pitcher in baseball.

PEDRO GUERRERO
outfielder
Los Angeles Dodgers

Born June 29, 1956 in San Pedro de Macoris, Dominican Republic

The Dominican Republic is a country in the Caribbean Sea south of Florida, where baseball is the Number 1 sport. Pedro Guerrero grew up there, playing baseball almost every day as a boy.

Just before he entered pro baseball in 1973, Guerrero was the best baseball player in his country with a .438 batting average in Legion baseball.

After five years learning in the minor leagues, Pedro became one of baseball's best power hitters. He hits a lot of home runs. He once hit 15 home runs in one month! No one has ever hit more than 18 home runs in one month in baseball's history.

Pedro is a .300 hitter, too. He doesn't just hit home runs. In the 1981 World Series, he hit .333 and was a co-Most Valuable Player.

HE HAS TO PLAY—Pedro is such a good hitter he has to play. Manager Tommy Lasorda has played him at first base, second base, third base, and in the outfield. No matter who else plays, Guerrero is so good a hitter he has to play somewhere. Pedro likes the outfield best, however.

RON GUIDRY
pitcher
New York Yankees

Born August 28, 1950 in Lafayette, Louisiana
Attended Northside High School and the
University of Southwestern Louisiana.

Nickname: Louisiana Lightning

The New York Yankees are major league
baseball's all-time winningest team, and Ron
Guidry, their ace left-handed pitcher, is a real
winner, too.

When Guidry was a boy, he dreamed of one
day playing for the New York Yankees. But he
didn't even get to play baseball in high school. His
school didn't have a team, so he ran on the track
team. But when he went to college Ron played
baseball and was very good. He was good enough
and lucky enough to get to play for his favorite
team—the Yankees. Soon he was the best pitcher
in major league baseball. In 1978 he won 25 games
and once struck out 18 batters in one game!

THIS GUY IS TOUGH—You have to be strong
and determined to be a great pitcher and finish
games when you are tired. Guidry proved his
toughness when he once broke a finger catching
the ball, but still kept playing with his finger in a
splint. He didn't miss a pitching start.

TONY GWYNN
outfielder
San Diego Padres

Born May 9, 1959 in Los Angeles, California
Attended Poly Technical (San Diego) High
School and San Diego State University.

Tony Gwynn is a young star who is a player to
be reckoned with. In 1984 Gwynn played his first
full year with the Padres. He led the league in
hitting with a .351 average. He also led the league
in hits (213) and multiple-hit games (69). He was
the first player in Padre history to get more than
200 hits in a season.

Tony was the epitome of consistency. He hit
.351 in the first half of the season and .352 in the
second half. And he didn't strike out much. He led
all big league hitters in the category of fewest
strikeouts (23) per times at bat (606).

In 1985, Gwynn hit .317 and was fourth in the
National League.

A HOOP STAR TOO—Gwynn went to college
at San Diego State. There, he played both baseball
and basketball. He was a starting guard on the
Aztec basketball team and good enough so that the
San Diego Clippers of the NBA drafted him. He
chose to play baseball, however.

RICKEY HENDERSON
outfielder
New York Yankees

Born December 25, 1958 in Chicago, Illinois
Attended Oakland (California) Technical High
School.

When major league baseball was first played,
players were fast and almost never hit home runs.
Then came Babe Ruth and everyone started to hit
home runs. Teams used players that hit home runs
instead of fast runners.

But that changed again, and teams started
looking for runners who were very fast. The
teams also hoped the players could hit some home
runs.

Rickey Henderson showed them how it could
be done. He was a great high school athlete. Then
he started pro baseball and showed he could do
everything well—run fast, hit home runs, and get
on base.

But the thing he does best is steal bases. In
1980 he stole 100 bases. In 1982 he stole 130 and
set the modern major league record. In 1983 he
stole 108.

HE IS THE BEST—Famous manager Earl
Weaver says of Henderson: "The guy is simply the
most gifted all-around player in the game."

25

TOM HERR
second baseman
St. Louis Cardinals

Born April 4, 1956 in Lancaster, Pennsylvania
Attended Hampfield (Landisville, Pennsylvania)
High School.

Being a major league baseball player, even an
All-Star like Tom Herr of the St. Louis Cardinals,
isn't all the glamour, excitement, and big dollars.
Sometimes it is painful injuries, operations, and
long hours of exercise to be able to play again.

That's the story of Tom Herr, one of baseball's
best infielders. In 1981 he had only five errors in
590 chances at second base, the best performance
by a Cardinal ever. But in 1982 he hurt his right
knee, and it had to be operated on. In 1983 he hurt
his left knee, working out, and it too had to be
operated on. Then he hurt his left knee again, and
spent six weeks in a cast, followed by swimming
and bicycling exercise.

Tom Herr has paid his dues. Now he is playing
All-Star baseball again, playing in the World
Series, and hitting .300.

A SINGLES HITTER—Herr is a fine switch-
hitter. He hits mostly singles. In fact, he was at bat
1,161 times before he hit his first home run! In
1985 he hit eight home runs.

DON MATTINGLY
first baseman
New York Yankees

Born April 20, 1961 in Evansville, Indiana
Attended Evansville (Indiana) Memorial High
School.

Don Mattingly is a batting champion. He is one
of the best hitters in baseball today. In 1984 he was
the American League's best hitter with a .343
average. In 1985 he led the league in doubles, runs
batted in, and game-winning hits. He hit 35 home
runs.

But a hitter like Mattingly still has to work
hard to learn to be a good hitter. And he has to go
to other people to learn. "The kid got smarter,
grew a little more physically, and then we helped
his power by getting him to hit more off his back
foot," says Yogi Berra. Yankee manager Lou
Piniella actually did the teaching. "He taught me a
better way to swing through the ball, so that I
wasn't pulling up short and losing some of my
power," Mattingly says.

A NICE GUY—Batting, Don Mattingly is very
aggressive. He tries very hard. But off the field he
is soft-spoken, polite, and down-to-earth. In high
school he played Little League, Babe Ruth, and
American Legion baseball. His brother, Randy, was
a pro football player.

WILLIE McGEE
outfielder
St. Louis Cardinals

Born November 2, 1958 in San Francisco,
California
Attended Diablo Valley Junior College.

Nickname: E. T.

Power is one way to be a great baseball player.
Speed is another. Willie McGee is one of the
fastest players in baseball. He plays center field.
That means he has to cover the largest amount of
space on the field, running deep into the gaps
between the outfielders so rolling hits don't
become doubles and triples.

"I give 110 percent every night and the people
here who see you like that," McGee says.

It took Willie a long time to become a major
league player. He thought he would never make it.
But, after six years in the minor leagues, he did it.
Now he is a switch-hitting, multi-talented All-Star
and Golden Glove player. He can do it all.

INJURY PREVENTION—McGee's father is a
deacon in the Pentecostal church. Each year he
annoints Willie's hands and feet with sacred oil and
blesses them to keep them from injury.

DALE MURPHY
outfielder
Atlanta Braves

Born March 12, 1956 in Portland, Oregon
Attended Woodrow Wilson High School in
Portland and Brigham Young University.

Dale Murphy is almost too good to be true. In
fact, some people kid him about being too nice a
guy. Murphy just smiles and continues to do
whatever people ask—he never refuses an
autograph request. He gives lots of speeches to
children. And he works for many charities. He is a
man who goes to church, is devoted to his family
(he has three sons), and doesn't drink, smoke, or
swear.

Murphy also is a great baseball player. He is a
rarity—the complete player. He can run, hit,
throw, and catch as well as anyone. He has twice
been named the Most Valuable Player. He hits lots
of home runs, 37 in 1985. And at 6 feet 5 inches,
215 pounds, he is a handsome man, too.

IS HE A LEFTY OR RIGHTY?—Murphy bats
and throws right-handed. But he writes and eats
left-handed! "I don't know how it happened, it just
worked out that way," he says.

EDDIE MURRAY
first baseman
Baltimore Orioles

Born February 24, 1956 in Los Angeles,
California

Attended Locke High School in Los Angeles
and California State University in Los Angeles.

Nickname: Mr. September

Eddie Murray has been in major league baseball
for nine years. Each year he seems to get better.
He has always been right around a .300 hitter.
There's never been any question about his power,
and because he's a switch-hitter he can play every
day against almost any pitcher.

Nothing seems to bother Murray. He's never
hit less than .283 and many people consider him to
be the best all-around player in the game today.

EDDIE LEARNED EARLY—One of 12
children, all five of the Murray boys played
professional baseball. And Eddie played on a great
high school baseball team. There were some future
major leaguers on his team: Eddie, his brother
Rich, Gary Alexander, St. Louis Cardinals great
shortstop Ozzie Smith, and Darrell Jackson, who
played with the Twins. Jackson, Murray, and Smith
were tri-captains their senior year. What a team!

DAN QUISENBERRY
pitcher
Kansas City Royals

Born February 7, 1953 in Santa Monica,
California
Attended Costa Mesa High School, Orange
Coast College, and LaVerne (California) College.

Nickname: The Australian

You might wonder about Dan Quisenberry's
nickname. He's called the Australian because his
pitches come from Down Under. He is a sidearm
pitcher. He throws with his hand beside or below
his body, not above it as most pitchers.

Quisenberry likes the way he pitches. He is a
reliever. "I like to pitch a lot," he says. "At first I
was a pure sinker baller, but I've learned to change
speeds and throw knuckleballs."

Quisenberry is so good he is the best relief
pitcher in the American League. In 1985 he had 37
saves. In 1984 he had 44 and in '83 he had 45. Five
times he has led the league or tied for the lead.

DAN Q. NEEDS HELP—Quisenberry is a
great pitcher, but he has lots of balls hit on the
ground to his infielders. He appreciates the work
of the good Kansas City Royals infielders who
turn his ground balls into outs.

CAL RIPKEN JR.

shortstop

Baltimore Orioles

Born August 24, 1960 in Havre de Grace, Maryland

Attended Aberdeen High School in Aberdeen, Maryland.

You cannot talk about Cal Ripken Jr. without talking about his father, Cal Ripken Sr. Cal is named after his father, and he is following in his father's footsteps.

Cal Ripken Jr. is the Baltimore Orioles shortstop. His father, Cal Sr., is the Baltimore Orioles third base coach.

In 1982, Cal Jr. was the Rookie of the Year. In 1983 he was the American League Most Valuable Player. And in 1984, only a little more than two years after he started major league baseball, he signed a $4 million dollar contract. Now Cal Jr. is a star.

BILLY IS COMING—Cal's younger brother, Billy, is also a baseball player. He is playing minor league baseball, trying to get to the major leagues. He is also a shortstop. Cal Jr. says he'd be glad to move to third base to make room for Billy. That would make *three* Ripkens on the Baltimore Orioles!

PETE ROSE
first baseman/manager
Cincinnati Reds

Born April 14, 1941 in Anderson Ferry, Ohio
Attended Western Hills (Cincinnati) High
School.

Nickname: Charlie Hustle

Pete Rose works hard at baseball, the game he
loves. He always wanted to be a baseball player.
His father taught him to be a switch-hitter so he
can bat left- or right-handed. Pete has played for
23 years. He has played in more winning games
than any player in history. He has more hits than
any player in history. He broke Ty Cobb's record
in 1985. And now he is the first baseman and the
manager of his favorite team, the Cincinnati Reds.

Rose is an old-fashioned kind of player. He
runs hard and plays hard, all the time. Even if his
team is far behind, he tries to win. "He's smart,"
says Ted Williams, one of the greatest hitters ever.
"He's durable, versatile, and a great contact hitter."

THE RECORD BOOK—Pete Rose knows all
his records, and he has dozens and dozens of
them. He can talk baseball all day with anyone.
There is only one thing in Rose's life, and that's
baseball. He was 44 years old in 1985, still setting
records. He is a marvel.

BRET SABERHAGEN
pitcher
Kansas City Royals

Born April 11, 1964 in Chicago Heights, Illinois
Attended Cleveland (Reseda, California) High
School.

Some baseball players are so good when they
are young, they become stars right away. We call
them superstars. If they are lucky and are not
injured, they can set records.

Bret Saberhagen is a superstar. Yet, he is only
21 years old. He has only pitched in the major
leagues for two years. But after the 1985 season
Saberhagen was voted the winner of the American
League Cy Young Award.

Saberhagen did it all in 1985. He was the
youngest American League pitcher in 31 years to
win 20 games. He led his team to the World Series,
and his Royals won.

WORLD SERIES HIGHLIGHTS—Saberhagen
really enjoyed the World Series. He was supposed
to pitch the last game. Each team had won three
times. This game was to decide the championship.
The day before, Saberhagen's wife gave birth to
their first child, a boy. Bret then pitched the game,
and won 11 to 0! He says he will never be able to
top that season.

RYNE SANDBERG
second baseman
Chicago Cubs

Born September 19, 1959 in Spokane, Washington
Attended North Central High School in Spokane.

Nickname: Ryno

No player in baseball history has ever had a season when he had 200 or more hits plus 20 or more doubles, triples, homers, and stolen bases. Ryne Sandberg came the closest to achieving that plateau, falling short by just one home run and one triple in 1984. That's the season Ryno emerged as one of baseball's premier all-around players. He won the league's Most Valuable Player Award and also earned a Gold Glove at second base for the second consecutive year.

Consistency and completeness are Sandberg's marks. He does everything well day after day—the mark of a real ball player. And Sandberg really does do it all, offense and defense.

OFF THE FIELD—When he isn't playing baseball, Sandberg lives in Tempe, Arizona. His hobbies are hunting, fishing, hiking, playing tennis, and listening to music. In high school, he was a very good football and basketball player, too.

OZZIE SMITH
shortstop
St. Louis Cardinals

Born December 26, 1954 in Mobile, Alabama
Attended Locke High School in Los Angeles
and was graduated from California State Poly.

Nickname: The Wizard of Oz

A great baseball team has to have its greatness
up the middle. It has to have good players at
catcher, pitcher, second base, shortstop, and
centerfield. Ozzie Smith gives his Cardinals the
premier defensive shortstop in baseball. Ozzie is
just the best—that's all there is to it.

Since 1980, when he was a San Diego Padre,
Ozzie has been the Gold Glove shortstop in the
National League. He is an All-Star player
appropriately nicknamed The Wizard of Oz
because of the way he fields, almost magically.

Ozzie's trademark is a back flip. He performs
just before the season opening game each year,
and at special occasions. He did his back flip at the
1985 World Series.

HELPING OTHERS—Ozzie Smith helps
others. He has a program to teach baseball to
children in juvenile halls in cities all over the
country. He also serves on the President's Council
for Drug Abuse.

DARRYL STRAWBERRY
outfielder
New York Mets

Born March 12, 1962 in Los Angeles, California
Attended Crenshaw High School (Los Angeles).

Darryl Strawberry was always a good baseball
player. He grew up in Southern California, where
many great baseball players grow up. He was one
of the best. But when he started to play
professional baseball, he struggled to be good.

After three years in the minors, still learning,
Darryl started playing for the Mets. But still he
was not good. After a month, he was only hitting
.161. Then teammate Keith Hernandez joined the
team, and Darryl started to relax. Soon he was
hitting well and playing well. By the end of the
year he was Rookie of the Year with the most
home runs by a left-hand hitter, the most home
runs by a rookie, and the most runs batted in.

AN EARLY START—The first time Darryl
Strawberry played catch in the park where his
brothers played baseball, a man stopped him and
said, "You can play in the major leagues someday."

Darryl was only 10 years old. But he
remembered. "I kept remembering . . . by the time
I was in high school, I was pretty sure that's what
I wanted to do."

FERNANDO VALENZUELA
pitcher
Los Angeles Dodgers

Born November 11, 1960 in Etchohuaquila, Mexico

Fernando Valenzuela is from Mexico. His 12 older brothers and sisters taught him to play baseball. He could only play pitcher when his six older brothers let him. But when he was only 15 years old, Fernando signed a contract to become a professional baseball player. He had to leave home to do it.

In 1981 he was a rookie, but the Los Angeles Dodgers asked him to pitch the season-opening game, a real honor. He surprised everyone by winning. He didn't allow the other team a run—a shutout! Then he won again. And again. Soon he had won eight games in a row and he was a superstar. At the end of the year, even though he was only 20 years old and the youngest player in major league baseball, he was one of the best. He was the Rookie of the Year in the National League and the Cy Young Award winner.

WORLD SERIES CHAMPION—Fernando's rookie year was important because his team, the Los Angeles Dodgers, played in the World Series. They lost the first two games. Then Valenzuela got to pitch. He won, and the team went on to win the World Series!

DAVE WINFIELD
outfielder
New York Yankees

Born October 3, 1951 in St. Paul, Minnesota Attended St. Paul Central High School and was graduated from the University of Minnesota.

Dave Winfield is a big man. He stands 6 feet 6 inches and weighs 220 pounds. With all that size and power he can hit the ball as hard as anyone ever has. He is one of the best long-ball hitters in baseball. He has had an outstanding 12-year career with the San Diego Padres and the Yankees.

At the University of Minnesota he played basketball and baseball. He was a pitcher and outfielder in baseball, winning 13 of 14 games as a senior. When he graduated, the Padres wanted him to play baseball, the Minnesota Vikings wanted him to play football, and two professional basketball teams wanted him to play basketball. He chose baseball and it was the right choice.

WINFIELD HELPS CHILDREN—Dave started the David M. Winfield Foundation to work with youth groups and make contributions to the community. He has helped many kids. He has given money for college scholarships. Dave Winfield makes a lot of money playing baseball, but he gives some of it to others who need help.

WORLD SERIES HISTORY

Year	Teams (League)	Games Won
1903	Pittsburgh Pirates (NL)	3
	Boston Red Sox (AL)	5
1904	No World Series was played.	
1905	New York Giants (NL)	4
	Philadelphia Athletics (AL)	1
1906	Chicago Cubs (NL)	2
	Chicago White Sox (AL)	4
1907	Chicago Cubs (NL)	4
	Detroit Tigers (AL)..............................	0
1908	Chicago Cubs (NL)	4
	Detroit Tigers (AL)..............................	1
1909	Pittsburgh Pirates (NL)	4
	Detroit Tigers (AL)..............................	3
1910	Chicago Cubs (NL)	1
	Philadelphia Athletics (AL)	4
1911	New York Giants (NL)	2
	Philadelphia Athletics (AL)	4
1912	New York Giants (NL)	3
	Boston Red Sox (AL)	4
1913	New York Giants (NL)	1
	Philadelphia Athletics (AL)	4
1914	Boston Braves (NL).............................	4
	Philadelphia Athletics (AL)	0
1915	Philadelphia Phillies (NL)	1
	Boston Red Sox (AL)	4
1916	Brooklyn Dodgers (NL)	1
	Boston Red Sox (AL)	4
1917	New York Giants (NL)	2
	Chicago White Sox (AL)	4
1918	Chicago Cubs (NL)	2
	Boston Red Sox (AL)	4
1919	Cincinnati Reds (NL)	5
	Chicago White Sox (AL)	3
1920	Brooklyn Dodgers (NL)	2
	Cleveland Indians (AL)	5
1921	New York Giants (NL)	5
	New York Yankees (AL)	3

1922	New York Giants (NL)	4
	New York Yankees (AL)	0
1923	New York Giants (NL)	2
	New York Yankees (AL)	4
1924	New York Giants (NL)	3
	Washington Senators (AL)	4
1925	Pittsburgh Pirates (NL)	4
	Washington Senators (AL)	3
1926	St. Louis Cardinals (NL)	4
	New York Yankees (AL)	3
1927	Pittsburgh Pirates (NL)	0
	New York Yankees (AL)	4
1928	St. Louis Cardinals (NL)	0
	New York Yankees (AL)	4
1929	Chicago Cubs (NL)	1
	Philadelphia Athletics (AL)	4
1930	St. Louis Cardinals (NL)	2
	Philadelphia Athletics (AL)	4
1931	St. Louis Cardinals (NL)	4
	Philadelphia Athletics (AL)	3
1932	Chicago Cubs (NL)	0
	New York Yankees (AL)	4
1933	New York Giants (NL)	4
	Washington Senators (AL)	1
1934	St. Louis Cardinals (NL)	4
	Detroit Tigers (AL)	3
1935	Chicago Cubs (NL)	2
	Detroit Tigers (AL)	4
1936	New York Giants (NL)	2
	New York Yankees (AL)	4
1937	New York Giants (NL)	1
	New York Yankees (AL)	4
1938	Chicago Cubs (NL)	0
	New York Yankees (AL)	4
1939	Cincinnati Reds (NL)	0
	New York Yankees (AL)	4
1940	Cincinnati Reds (NL)	4
	Detroit Tigers (AL)	3
1941	Brooklyn Dodgers (NL)	1
	New York Yankees (AL)	4
1942	St. Louis Cardinals (NL)	4
	New York Yankees (AL)	1
1943	St. Louis Cardinals (NL)	1
	New York Yankees (AL)	4
1944	St. Louis Cardinals (NL)	4
	St. Louis Browns (AL)	2

1945	Chicago Cubs (NL)	3
	Detroit Tigers (AL)	4
1946	St. Louis Cardinals (NL)	4
	Boston Red Sox (AL)	3
1947	Brooklyn Dodgers (NL)	3
	New York Yankees (AL)	4
1948	Boston Braves (NL)...........................	2
	Cleveland Indians (AL)	4
1949	Brooklyn Dodgers (NL)	1
	New York Yankees (AL)	4
1950	Philadelphia Phillies (NL)	0
	New York Yankees (AL)	4
1951	New York Giants (NL)	2
	New York Yankees (AL)	4
1952	Brooklyn Dodgers (NL)	3
	New York Yankees (AL)	4
1953	Brooklyn Dodgers (NL)	2
	New York Yankees (AL)	4
1954	New York Giants (NL)	4
	Cleveland Indians (AL)	0
1955	Brooklyn Dodgers (NL)	4
	New York Yankees (AL)	3
1956	Brooklyn Dodgers (NL)	3
	New York Yankees (AL)	4
1957	Milwaukee Braves (NL)	4
	New York Yankees (AL)	3
1958	Milwaukee Braves (NL)	3
	New York Yankees (AL)	4
1959	Los Angeles Dodgers (NL)	4
	Chicago White Sox (AL)	2
1960	Pittsburgh Pirates (NL)	4
	New York Yankees (AL)	3
1961	Cincinnati Reds (NL)	1
	New York Yankees (AL)	4
1962	San Francisco Giants (NL)	3
	New York Yankees (AL)	4
1963	Los Angeles Dodgers (NL)	4
	New York Yankees (AL)	0
1964	St. Louis Cardinals (NL)	4
	New York Yankees (AL)	3
1965	Los Angeles Dodgers (NL)	4
	Minnesota Twins (AL)	3
1966	Los Angeles Dodgers (NL)	0
	Baltimore Orioles (AL)	4
1967	St. Louis Cardinals (NL)	4
	Boston Red Sox (AL)	3

1968	St. Louis Cardinals (NL) 3
	Detroit Tigers (AL) 4
1969	New York Mets (NL) 4
	Baltimore Orioles (AL) 1
1970	Cincinnati Reds (NL) 1
	Baltimore Orioles (AL) 4
1971	Pittsburgh Pirates (NL) 4
	Baltimore Orioles (AL) 3
1972	Cincinnati Reds (NL) 3
	Oakland Athletics (AL) 4
1973	New York Mets (NL) 3
	Oakland Athletics (AL) 4
1974	Los Angeles Dodgers (NL) 1
	Oakland Athletics (AL) 4
1975	Cincinnati Reds (NL) 4
	Boston Red Sox (AL) 3
1976	Cincinnati Reds (NL) 4
	New York Yankees (AL) 0
1977	Los Angeles Dodgers (NL) 2
	New York Yankees (AL) 4
1978	Los Angeles Dodgers (NL) 2
	New York Yankees (AL) 4
1979	Pittsburgh Pirates (NL) 4
	Baltimore Orioles (AL) 3
1980	Philadelphia Phillies (NL) 4
	Kansas City Royals (AL) 2
1981	Los Angeles Dodgers (NL) 4
	New York Yankees (AL) 2
1982	St. Louis Cardinals (NL) 4
	Milwaukee Brewers (AL) 3
1983	Philadelphia Phillies (NL) 1
	Baltimore Orioles (AL) 4
1984	San Diego Padres (NL) 1
	Detroit Tigers (AL) 4
1985	St. Louis Cardinals (NL) 3
	Kansas City Royals (AL) 4

NATIONAL LEAGUE

EASTERN DIVISION

Chicago Cubs, 1876
  World Series winner, 1907, 1908
  World Series loser, 1906, 1910, 1918, 1929, 1932, 1935,
1938, 1945
  Championship Series winner, none
  Championship Series loser, 1984
  Team colors: royal blue, red, and white
  Stadium: Wrigley Field, 37,242, grass

Montreal Expos, 1969
  World Series winner, none
  Championship Series winner, none
  Championship Series loser, 1981
  Team colors: scarlet, white, royal blue, and blue
  Stadium: Olympic Stadium, 59,149, artificial turf

New York Mets, 1962
  World Series winner, 1969
  World Series loser, 1973
  Championship Series winner, 1969, 1973
  Team colors: white, orange, and blue
  Stadium: Shea Stadium, 55,601, grass

Philadelphia Phillies, 1876
  World Series winner, 1980
  World Series loser, 1915, 1950, 1983
  Championship Series winner, 1980, 1983
  Championship Series loser, 1976, 1977, 1978
  Team colors: crimson and white
  Stadium: Veterans Stadium, 66,744, artificial turf

Pittsburgh Pirates, 1876
   World Series winner, 1909, 1925, 1960, 1971, 1979
   World Series loser, 1903, 1927
   Championship Series winner, 1971, 1979
   Championship Series loser, 1970, 1972, 1974, 1975
   Team colors: white, black, and gold
   Stadium: Three Rivers Stadium, 58,429, artificial turf

St. Louis Cardinals, 1876
   World Series winner, 1926, 1931, 1934, 1942, 1944, 1946,
1964, 1967, 1982
   World Series loser, 1928, 1930, 1943, 1968, 1985
   Championship Series winner, 1982
   Team colors: scarlet, white, and navy
   Stadium: Busch Stadium, 50,222, artificial turf

WESTERN DIVISION

Atlanta Braves, 1966 (Boston Braves, 1901-1952; Milwaukee
Braves, 1953-1965)
   World Series winner, none
   Championship Series winner, none
   Championship Series loser, 1969, 1982
   Team colors: blue, red, and white
   Stadium: Atlanta Fulton County Stadium, 53,046, grass

Cincinnati Reds, 1869
   World Series winner, 1919, 1940, 1975, 1976
   World Series loser, 1939, 1961, 1970, 1972
   Championship Series winner, 1970, 1972, 1975, 1976
   Championship Series loser, 1973, 1979
   Team colors: scarlet and white
   Stadium: Riverfront Stadium, 52,392, artificial turf

Houston Astros, 1962
World Series winner, none
Championship Series winner, none
Championship Series loser, 1980
Team colors: orange, navy, yellow, burnt orange, and white
Stadium: The Astrodome, 45,000, artificial turf

Los Angeles Dodgers, 1958 (Brooklyn Bridegroom, 1890-1898; Brooklyn Superbas, 1899-1910; Brooklyn Dodgers, 1911-1957)
World Series winner, 1955, 1959, 1965, 1981
World Series loser, 1963, 1966, 1974, 1977, 1978
Championship Series winner, 1974, 1977, 1978, 1981
Championship Series loser, 1983
Team colors: royal blue, white, and red
Stadium: Dodger Stadium, 56,000, grass

San Diego Padres, 1969
World Series winner, none
World Series loser, 1984
Championship Series winner, 1984
Team colors: brown, orange, and white
Stadium: San Diego/Jack Murphy Stadium, 58,396, grass

San Francisco Giants, 1958 (New York Giants, 1876-1957)
World Series winner, none
World Series loser, 1962
Championship Series winner, none
Championship Series loser, 1971
Team colors: black, orange, and white
Stadium: Candlestick Park, 58,000, grass

AMERICAN LEAGUE

EASTERN DIVISION

Baltimore Orioles, 1954 (St. Louis Browns, 1902-1953)
World Series winner, 1966, 1970, 1983
World Series loser, 1969, 1971, 1979
Championship Series winner, 1969, 1970, 1971, 1979, 1983
Championship Series loser, 1973, 1974
Team colors: red-orange and black
Stadium: Memorial Stadium, 53,196, grass

Boston Red Sox, 1901
World Series winner, 1903, 1913, 1915, 1916, 1918
World Series loser, 1946, 1967, 1975
Championship Series winner, 1975
Team colors: red, white, and blue
Stadium: Fenway Park, 33,583, grass

Cleveland Indians, 1901
World Series winner, 1920, 1948
World Series loser, 1954
Championship Series winner, none
Team colors: white, red, and navy
Stadium: Cleveland Stadium, 74,208, grass

Detroit Tigers, 1901
World Series winner, 1935, 1945, 1968, 1984
World Series loser, 1907, 1908, 1909, 1934, 1940
Championship Series winner, 1984
Championship Series loser, 1972
Team colors: orange, white, and navy
Stadium: Tiger Stadium, 52,806, grass

Milwaukee Brewers, 1970
   World Series winner, none
   World Series loser, 1982
   Championship Series winner, 1982
   Team colors: royal blue, white, and gold
   Stadium: County Stadium, 53,192, grass

New York Yankees, 1903
   World Series winner, 1923, 1927, 1928, 1932, 1936, 1937,
1938, 1939, 1941, 1943, 1947, 1949, 1950, 1951, 1952, 1953,
1956, 1958, 1962, 1977, 1978
   World Series loser, 1921, 1922, 1926, 1942, 1955, 1957,
1960, 1961, 1963, 1964, 1976, 1981
   Championship Series winner, 1976, 1977, 1978, 1981
   Championship Series loser, 1980
   Team colors: navy and white
   Stadium: Yankee Stadium, 57,545, grass

Toronto Blue Jays, 1977
   World Series winner, none
   Championship Series winner, none
   Championship Series loser, 1985
   Team colors: white, blue, and dark blue
   Stadium: Exhibition Stadium, 43,737, artificial turf

WESTERN DIVISION

California Angels, 1961
   World Series winner, none
   Championship Series winner, none
   Championship Series loser, 1979, 1982
   Team colors: red, white, and navy
   Stadium: Anaheim Stadium, 65,158, grass

Chicago White Sox, 1900
World Series winner, 1906, 1917
World Series loser, 1919, 1959
Championship Series winner, none
Championship Series loser, 1983
Team colors: white, navy, and red
Stadium: Comisky Park, 44,087, grass

Kansas City Royals, 1969
World Series winner, 1985
World Series loser, 1980
Championship Series winner, 1980, 1985
Championship Series loser, 1976, 1977, 1978, 1984
Team colors: royal blue and white
Stadium: Royal Stadium, 40,635, artificial turf

Minnesota Twins, 1954 (Washington Senators, 1901-1953)
World Series winner, none
World Series loser, 1965
Championship Series winner, 1965
Championship Series loser, 1969, 1970
Team colors: scarlet, white, and blue
Stadium: Hubert H. Humphrey Metrodome, 55,122,
artificial turf

Oakland A's, 1968 (Philadelphia Athletics, 1901-1955; Kansas
City A's, 1955-1967)
World Series winner, 1973, 1974
World Series loser, 1972
Championship Series winner, 1972, 1973, 1974
Championship Series loser, 1971, 1975, 1981
Team colors: green, gold, and white
Stadium: Oakland Coliseum, 50,219, grass

Seattle Mariners, 1977
World Series winner, none
Championship Series winner, none
Team colors: mariner blue, gold, and white
Stadium: The Kingdome, 59,438, artificial turf

Texas Rangers, 1972
World Series winner, none
Championship Series winner, none
Team colors: red, white, and blue
Stadium: Arlington Stadium, 43,508, grass

About the Author

Mike Herbert is a sports magazine editor. He has
been a writer and editor for twenty years. The
magazines he edits are written for sports fans. They are:
*Inside Sports, Auto Racing Digest, Basketball Digest, Basketball
Digest Yearbook, Bowling Digest, Football Digest, Football Digest
Yearbook, Hockey Digest,* and *Soccer Digest.*

Before he was a magazine editor, Mr. Herbert was a
high school English teacher and a football and basketball
coach. He grew up in Michigan and played sports in high
school and college. He has always loved all kinds of
sports. Today, he especially likes to play golf.

Mr. Herbert lives in Naperville, Illinois. He is married
and has two daughters. The whole family enjoys being
sports spectators and playing sports.

Mr. Herbert has written many magazine articles and
a book for Childrens Press in the Sports Stars series:
Mike Schmidt: The Human Vacuum Cleaner.